MW01688617

Youth Ministry Sketches

. . . that aren't LAME

by

Mike Massé

ISBN #0-9713711-8-0

Cover art: Toby Zintz
Back cover photo: "Tommy Boy" Dziekan
Cover layout: Zachary Miller
Book layout: Leo Ward

Published by: Ivan Press, a division of
Elim Publishing
1679 Dalton Road
Lima, NY 14485

Contact: info@elimpublishing.com
Home Page: www.elimpublishing.com

Dedication

At four very different stages of my Christian walk, there were four ministers there to encourage and support me no matter what else anyone said.

For this, I dedicate my first book to . . .

Michael Gaiotti,

David Bonadies,

Daniel Grimes,

and

Robert Rulewicz.

Acknowledgements

The only cliche you will find in this book...because it bears repeating often, is: Thanks to God. You gave me two of my biggest passions and giftings in youth ministry and writing.

Thanks to everyone that came up with creative concepts, collaborated with me, or just had a funny conversation that I ended up using: Patrick Fitzgerald, Steve Kaplan, Ben Levendusky, Frank Spadaro, TJ Steele, Dave Waite, and the "author unknown" who wrote "Entertaining Jesus" at least a decade and a half ago...and it hasn't gotten any less powerful through the years.

Thanks to Toby Zintz for his original art on the cover, and to Randy Johnson and Leo Ward for the publishing, design, and editing on this spectacular collection of humorous sketches.

Thanks to everyone who's ever acted in my sketches, especially "the" Christian DiNello (yes, most of the character names are the actor who originated the part), Michael "Black Hole" Paradis, and "they killed" Nick Bianca.

Thanks to John Massé, Michael Moore, and Sarah Toomey for sharpening my sense of humor over the years.

Thanks to my parents for signing me up to be a main character in the town Christmas play when I was five years old.

~ Mike Massé

Introduction

Youth Ministry Sketches . . . that aren't LAME

I've always liked sketches. I'll never forget my first year of volunteer youth ministry, at age 18. I was put in charge of picking out a drama from a book, recruiting actors, rehearsing, directing, playing the main character myself and finally, performing for the annual youth service in front of the congregation of 500 on Sunday morning. It was a "traditional" sketch (definition: one that everyone in church or at camp has seen before). Satan comes to a party and gets everyone in bondage to music, drinking, and drugs and then drags them all to hell. What happened afterward changed me. A 14-year-old kid came up and showed me his sneakers. They were covered with marker: symbols and words representing Marilyn Manson and other bands known for obscene and anti-God lyrics. He looked up and said, in effect: "I never realized what was behind the music. I'm throwing out these shoes, as well as all my CDs when I get home. Thanks." Since that conversation, the impact of a good sketch has been re-proven many times in front of my eyes. Humor loosens up a crowd, a new take on an old subject makes them think, and those powerful endings get them (and me) every time.

There's only one problem. That book of twenty dramas that I looked through that morning contained that one great skit, and nineteen that were incredibly lame. As I continued in youth ministry, I noticed that the majority of youth group sketch books were the same. You know what I'm talking about. Written by goodhearted people that mean well…and filled with corny jokes, predictable dialogue, and over-the-top preachiness. Youth groups of today roll their eyes at performing these – let alone inviting their unchurched friends to a service. Every sketch in this book has been tried and proven true. I've used them as object lessons to enhance messages, and kids remember them years later. Many of the jokes that found their way in came from teenagers (you will probably be able to guess which ones).

Some practical notes: As I did that day, feel free to change anything to make the skit more relevant to your audience. You know them better than I do. Never forget timing – that is, waiting for laughter to die down before saying the next line, ratcheting up the intensity when building to an important point, and so on. Practice and prayer are both necessary to achieve true performance success. None require more than the simplest of props.

And finally, my guarantee: You may get some people saying "This is unprecedented," but you will never get a youth saying "This is lame."

I pray many more sneakers get thrown out for Christ.

~ Mike Massé

Table of Contents

3-PART SERIES

EYE WITNESS

by Mike Massé

Over the years, I've noticed that most kids in youth groups know all the right things to say when "witnessing" – in situations that never occur in the real world. While the Bible does tell us to "always have an answer for those who ask us for the reason we hope," people aren't going to ask unless they first see a witness with their eyes.

CHARACTERS:
CHRISTIAN – newly born again young man
MIKE – Unchurched joker type
PATRICK – Unchurched joker type
SIGN CARRIER – to walk by with a sign

PROPS: mood ring, 200-page book (to be covered with a new title), frozen waffle, sign

---

CHRISTIAN (*to audience*): Hi, I'm Christian. Well, that's always been my name...but now it's my newfound faith in Jesus too. Wow. Ever since I became a Christian, I've been filled with so much joy and excitement. I can't wait to tell my two best friends about Jesus. They are great guys - but just like me until my newfound faith - they really don't have too much purpose in life. Hey, there they are now!

MIKE *and* PATRICK *walk up, oblivious to* CHRISTIAN'S *presence.*

MIKE (*to* PATRICK): Hey man, how are you feeling today?

PATRICK: Well, I think I feel pretty happy. But let me check my mood ring.

MIKE: It's turquoise.

PATRICK: Let me look up what that means (*takes out a 200-page "Guide to Deciphering Your Mood Ring" booklet*). Turquoise...oh, man, "apprehensive." I thought I was happy, but I guess I'm apprehensive.

MIKE: What could you possibly be apprehensive about?

PATRICK: Beats me. I don't even know what "apprehensive" means!

MIKE: I keep telling you, you need to listen to the teachers at school.

PATRICK: It's too hard. I don't think I can do it.

MIKE: You're always telling me you can't do things. I'm sick of you telling me you can't do things!

PATRICK: Well, it's not that I can't do it. I can do it…I just don't want to.

MIKE (*angrily*): No, you CAN do it, but you just don't want to!

PATRICK: That's what I said.

MIKE: Uh…yeah. I'm bored. What can we do?

PATRICK: Well, they're showing the new Star Wars down at the movie theater.

MIKE: Dude, we already saw that, remember?

PATRICK: Yeah, it was great! But let's go back and mess with the geeks who camp outside the movies dressed like Darth Vader and Chewbacca.

MIKE: Yeah, we should go dressed up as Spider-Man and the Hulk…and talk about fulfilling our quest to be the Lord of the Rings. Heh-heh, just imagine their reaction.

PATRICK: Yeah, and then we'll whip out those collectible lightsabers and act all ticked off when it doesn't actually shoot out a green beam. "You've all been fooled!"

MIKE: Wait, those don't work? I paid $400 for mine! I can't believe you said that!

PATRICK (*angry*): Oh yeah? Wanna fight?

MIKE (*furious, pointing at Patrick*): Those are fighting words!

CHRISTIAN (*interrupting*): Hey guys, I've got some good news! I'm a Christian now.

Their anger turns to confusion. They look at each other.

PATRICK: Dude, you've always been Christian.

MIKE: I mean, there was that one period in elementary school where you insisted we call you "Jenny." Remember how every day you wore an extra long-sleeved shirt on your head so you'd look like a girl with long hair?

CHRISTIAN: Mike, that was you.

MIKE: Oh…yeah. Um…my point is, your name has always been Christian.

CHRISTIAN: I'm not talking about my name, I'm talking about my newfound faith in Jesus. That kind of Christian.

PATRICK: So…you're going to start going to confession and wearing robes and stuff?

CHRISTIAN: No, it's not that. This is going to sound weird and hard to believe, but…I actually have a relationship with Jesus. I pray, worship, and read in the Bible about how He lived. Yeah, I try to treat people like He did, too. I'm telling you, there's nothing like it. I have something to live for now! You should try it!

MIKE: Why should I become a Christian?

CHRISTIAN (*to audience*): I never thought about that. Well, I have to tell him something. What were those things they always told me at youth group?

CHRISTIAN (*to his friends*): Haven't you ever felt like there was an empty spot in your life?

PATRICK: Dude, my life is awesome. I just got this cool mood ring, and they have Mountain Dew Slurpees for the next month at 7-11.

CHRISTIAN: Okay, but haven't you ever thought about where you go when you die?

MIKE: No, I always thought I'd donate my body to science. You know, so they could study a perfect specimen. Of course I have! I'm going to . . .

CHRISTIAN: Well, um, Jesus is the answer to all your problems!

PATRICK: How can that be true? Pastor *(insert the name of your church's pastor)* has been a Christian for years, and he's losing all his hair…my biggest fear in life.

MIKE: Yeah, bro, all your arguments are coming up pretty lame.

CHRISTIAN (*to audience*): Mike and Patrick are right. I can't put into words the way Jesus has changed my life. What is it that Jesus said? Love each other…be known by your fruit… Go your way and sin no more…wow, He really knew what He was talking about! I know I'll never be perfect, but I am going to try my hardest to spend time with God every day, and then go out and glorify Him with my thoughts, words, and actions.

CHRISTIAN (*to his friends*): You guys watch. You'll see how much I've changed, thanks to God's work in me. I don't care if it takes 3 years!

SIGN CARRIER *walks by with a sign that says "3 years later."*

MIKE: Well, Christian, you really have showed us something over these last 3 years. You haven't been perfect, but you really have tried your hardest to treat everyone, especially us, as kindly as possible. You prayed and read your Bible, just like you said you would. You helped the less fortunate, worked hard and honestly at school, and, I have to be honest…you can take a lot of abuse without losing your temper

PATRICK: Yeah…remember last summer when every time we saw him, we threw frozen waffles at him and called him a flamer?

MIKE: That's my point…when September rolled around and we got tired of that, he was still our friend. Christian, it's obvious you know the Bible, love God, and love your neighbor as yourself. How can I be saved?

PATRICK: Yeah, how can we be saved?

CHRISTIAN (*to audience*): See, all the prayer and patience is worth it. That's what being a true witness is all about.

He picks up his Bible and turns to pray with his friends, turning his back to the audience for the first time. A frozen waffle is stuck to the back of his shirt.

The End

TAMING THE TONGUE

by Mike Massé

One of the biggest struggles in every youth group I've ever seen is self-control over what comes out of our mouths. The Bible says if we don't do this, everything else is for show. This sketch exaggerates that point, and works great with a message on James 2 and watching our mouths.

CHARACTERS:
CHRISTIAN
UNPOPULAR GIRL
UNPOPULAR BOY
SCIENCE TEACHER/YOUTH LEADER
JESUS

PROPS: Toothbrush, Bible

CHRISTIAN *walks down the hallway of his school. He is waving his Bible around, clearly acting the part of the "holy Christian teenager."*

CHRISTIAN: Hallelujah, praise the Lord. Man, youth group was awesome last night. I can't wait for everyone to see how much I love Jesus. I'm the best Christian ever!

UNPOPULAR GIRL *approaches.*

UG: Hi, Christian.

CHRISTIAN: Did I just hear something? Because I know you're not talking to me. Don't you know that the losers use the other hallway? There's a reason for that…we can't stand to look at your ugly outfits and haircuts! You don't even deserve to live!

As he says each insult, UG *doubles over as in pain and reacts as if she's been poisoned. At the word "live," she falls to the ground and dies.* CHRISTIAN *steps over her body, shakes his head, and continues down the hallway, waving his Bible.*

CHRISTIAN: I'm not going to let something stupid like that steal the joy of the Lord! I can't wait to witness to all my friends!

UNPOPULAR BOY *approaches.*

UB: What's up, Christian?

CHRISTIAN: What's up…loser! Hey, ever heard of something called Tic-Tacs? Obviously not, otherwise you might even have a friend! With breath like yours, you might want to think about not breathing at all! Why don't you just drop dead!

As he says each insult, UB *doubles over as in pain and reacts as if he's been poisoned. At the word "dead," he falls to the ground and dies.* CHRISTIAN *steps over his body, shakes his head, and continues down the hallway, waving his Bible. A leader from youth group who also works as a teacher at the public school steps into the hall.*

SCIENCE TEACHER/YOUTH LEADER: Hey Christian, what's going on?

CHRISTIAN: Hey, Mr. M! I can't wait to witness about Jesus to all my cool friends.

YL: Do you realize you just killed two people with your rude comments? Is that what Jesus would want?

CHRISTIAN (*hangs his head*): No, I guess not. (*Looks up*) How did this happen?

YL: Well, James 2:8 says the tongue is full of deadly poison… and also says this – "Out of the same mouth comes praise and cursing. My brothers, this should not be."

CHRISTIAN: Can we pray together that Jesus will make my poison tongue clean again?

YL: Absolutely!

As they pray together, JESUS *appears with a toothbrush. He brushes* CHRISTIAN'S *mouth, and an obvious change comes over the young man.* JESUS *motions toward the two dead bodies before heading back to Heaven.*

YL: You know what you need to do now.

CHRISTIAN (*walking over to the bodies*). I'm sorry for what I said. I love you! Jesus loves you! Come back to life and come to youth group with me!

The two teenagers spring back to life. All three put their arms around each other, and walk out singing "Cumbaya" (or "Lord I Lift Your Name on High," whatever blatantly spiritual song the audience will know). The youth leader/teacher smiles and nods proudly.

The End

DWAYNE'S WORLD

by Frank Spadaro and Mike Massé

This is a perfect sketch for a youth service on Sunday morning at 'big church.' Adults that have never heard of "Wayne's World" crack up when they see how adolescents interpret the Proverbs of Solomon.

CHARACTERS:

DWAYNE – Should be played by a male age 17-30

MICHAEL – A legitimate middle school student…if one of your group is actually home-schooled, and the audience knows this, you are looking at comedic gold

BETH – A girl of any age

MUSICIAN who can play the guitar and sing the theme song a la "Wayne's World"

PROPS: A couch (chairs can be substituted), 'big hair' wig and mustache for Dwayne, sticks for both to air drum during the theme song, twenty dollar bill, bottled water, signs for the Bible verses (or you can display them on a screen with an overhead or projector).

THEME SONG: Dwayne's World! Dwayne's World! Party time! Excellent! Woo-woo-woo-woo!

The guys run on stage during the song, high-five, air drum, and sit down. (During every playing of the song they will air drum and exchange high-fives).

DWAYNE CAMPBELL: Hello, and welcome to Dwayne's World! I'm your excellent host, Dwayne Campbell, and this is my sidekick Michael Peterson.

MICHAEL PETERSON: Party on, Dwayne.

DC: Party on, Michael. Just to tell you a bit about ourselves, we are both middle school students in the community. I attend (*name of a community school*), and Michael here goes to... Pittsburgh?

MP: No, PIT!

DC: PIT?

MP: Yes. Peterson Institute of Technology.

DWAYNE *gives him a confused look.*

MP: I'm home schooled, okay? At least I haven't been in middle school for 8 years!

DC: Hey, you're just jealous of my sweet mustache. Besides, there's nothing wrong with being home schooled. You get to be valedictorian, homecoming king AND queen, student council president…and you're always bragging about being captain of the football team.

MP: Yeah, in your face, Dara!

DC: Way to show your 8-year-old sister who's the man. Anyway, I've been doing my "top ten" show on local cable for the last year, and ratings are at an all-time low. The station manager told me I'd better get some more viewers, quick! Everybody knows that Christians watch more TV than anyone, so I got myself a Christian sidekick – Michael here.

MP: I invited him to broadcast live from (*name of church or venue*) this morning.

DC: Well, I had never been to church in my life…so I prayed about it. But Batman didn't even answer me!

MP: God, man…you're supposed to pray to God!

DC: Oh, right. Party on.

MP: Anyway, this day marks a new high point for Christian television – Dwayne will be going over the top ten Proverbs of all time!

DC: Yeah, and since I don't actually know what a "Proverb" is, I invited the most knowledgeable Bible scholar I know…let's have a big churchly welcome for Beth!

The theme song plays again as BETH *enters. She sets down her signs (if used) and bottled water, and looks around.*

BETH: Hey guys, um, great place you got here, Dwayne.

DC: Thanks, I decorated myself.

B: That's wonderful. Are you ready to start?

REVISED THEME SONG: Dwayne's World! Top Ten! Proverbs! Woo-woo-woo-woo!

B: Here's number 10: Proverbs 26:18 – "Like a madman shooting deadly arrows is the one who deceives his neighbor and says, 'I was only joking.'"

DC: Wait a minute. So, like, what are you supposed to say?

MP: Maybe, like, tell the truth?

DC (*thinking, then nodding as if it's the most profound thing he's ever heard)*: All right.

B: Number 9: Proverbs 20:1 – "Wine is a mocker, and beer a brawler. He who is led astray by them is not wise."

DC: I know a kid or two at school who aren't so wise.

MP: I am proud to say my school is 100% alcohol free!

They exchange yet another high-five as the audience laughs uproariously

B: Number 8: Proverbs 15:3 – "The eyes of the Lord are everywhere, keeping watch on the wicked and the good."

DC and MP (*doing an upper body dance*): Oh, you better watch out, you better not cry, you better not pout, I'm telling you why!

B: Why?

DC: Check your Proverbs, dude.

B: Number 7: Proverbs 12:1 – "Whoever loves discipline loves knowledge, but he who hates correction is stupid."

DC and MP (*nod slowly, look at each other, then turn to* BETH): NEXT!

B: Number 6: Proverbs 11:4 – "Wealth is worthless in the day of wrath, but righteousness delivers from death."

As she reads, MICHAEL *searches through his pockets and takes something out.*

DC: What are you doing?

MP: Hey man, here's that 20 bucks I owe you! (*Throws it at* DWAYNE)

DC (*throws it back at him*): I don't want it!

MP (*throws it offstage*): Get it out of here!

B: Um, are you guys ready to go on?

MP: Yeah, please.

DC: Hey, look over there!

DWAYNE *points, and when* BETH *looks, he steals her bottled water.*

B: I didn't see anything. (DWAYNE *and* MICHAEL *laugh to themselves*.)

B: You guys are strange. Anyway, here's number 5: Proverbs 9:17 – "Stolen water is sweet; food eaten in secret is delicious." (*As she reads,* DWAYNE *chugs the water, and obviously enjoys it. When she notices, he quickly screws the cap back on.)*

B: Hey, is that my Poland Springs?

DC (*throws the water off stage*): I don't know what you're talking about.

B: Hmm, okay. Number 4: Proverbs 10:1 – "A wise son brings joy to his father, but a foolish son brings grief to his mother."

DC: A foolish son brings grief to his mother? Hey Michael, hasn't your mom been looking a little sad lately?

MICHAEL *hangs his head.*

DC: Oh, I'm sorry, man. I didn't mean it.

MP: I forgive you.

DC: You forgive me just like that? Wow.

MP: Hey, that's the love of Jesus.

DC (*after thinking for a few moments*): What must I do to be saved?

MP: Well, you can start by shaving off that mustache!

DC: I'll be back in a jiffy! (*runs off stage*)

B: Well, that was interesting. Would you like to move on now that the host has left?

MP: By all means, proceed.

B: Number 3: Proverbs 25:16 – "If you find honey…

MP (*interrupting*): Hey, I know this one. "If you find honey, eat just enough. Too much, and you'll spew!"

B: That's an interesting translation. Wouldst it be the King Michael Version?

MP: It wouldst!

B: I'll bet you don't know this one. Number 2: Proverbs 9:8 – "Do not rebuke a mocker or he will hate you; rebuke a wise man and he will love you.

MP: I see. Um, rebuke me.

B: What?

MP: I want to see if I pass the test. Rebuke me.

B: Okay. I rebuke you!

MP: I love you.

B: That's so sweet.

MP: I guess this means I'm a wise man.

B: More like a wise guy.

DWAYNE *comes back on stage, sans mustache.*

MP: Hey man, if I can get serious for a minute, I was just kidding about the mustache thing. All Jesus really wants you to do is give Him your life.

DC: I think I'll do that. It's great having you as a friend.

They walk offstage, hugging each other's shoulders. BETH *reads #1. As she reads, she looks around to make sure she's alone, grabs the drumsticks, and sits on the couch.*

B: And the number one Proverb of all time: Proverbs 13:20 – "He who walks with the wise, grows wise. But a companion of fools suffers harm."

BETH *sings the* REVISED THEME SONG:

Beth's World! Beth's World! Party time! Excellent! Woo-woo-woo-woo!

The End

THE AMAZING RACE

by Mike Massé, concept by Ben Levendusky

My friend Ben is gifted in physical comedy. One year at camp, he came up with a brief sketch where he threw himself all over the place, yet still rose to finish his "race." I liked it so much, I decided to develop it into this object lesson.

CHARACTERS:

ATHLETE 1 – Very cocky and self-reliant
ATHLETE 2 – Humble, loving Christian lad
ATTRACTIVE GIRLS (three to four)
ANNOUNCER

The sketch opens with the two young men on the starting line. ATHLETE 1 *is engaging in some serious trash talking.*

A1: I'm the man, you're a little girl. Look at the little girl. What a weak baby. A girl baby!

A2: Hey, you're pretty clever. What exactly is your point?

A1: Uh…I'm stronger than you!

A2: Heh, that's okay. God is my strength.

A1: Does your God have pythons like these? (*flexes his arms*)

A2: I'll be sure to ask when I get to Heaven.

A1: I'm not going to Heaven…I'm going to hell…I'll kick the devil in the head and take over. Soon, I'll open up my own chain of gyms. (*pause*) And an ice cream parlor: "Hell's Frozen Treats."

A2: I'm going to go over here now (*points down the starting line away from* A1 *and walks over*).

They begin the race. A1 *starts out by running over to* A2 *and pushing him down to the ground. As* A1 *runs like a true athletic specimen,* A2 *continues the race very clumsily. He finds humorous ways to trip and fall. This happens a total of seven times. At the end,* A1 *stops to talk to a group of attractive girls, and* A2 *wins the race. As* A2 *celebrates, the girls proceed to clothesline* A1 *down to the ground.*

ANNOUNCER: Proverbs 18:24 – “A righteous man may fall 7 times, yet he rises again. But the wicked are brought down by calamity."

The End

SUNDAY MORNING NITRO

by Mike Massé

This one is great for middle school kids who are into professional wrestling. Nothing really clever here, just a bunch of bodies flying around...so be aware of any kids who would be uncomfortable with that kind of physical contact. This was written a few years back, but these are parodies of wrestlers that most youth will still be familiar with.

CHARACTERS:
THE CROCK
BULK HOGAN
THE UNDERFAKER
OLDBERG
THE DEVIL – should wear black or red with red or white face paint
THE CHRISTIAN
ANNOUNCER 1
ANNOUNCER 2

PROPS: A Bible

ANNOUNCER 1: Ladies and gentlemen, welcome to tonight's pro wrestling event…a huge battle royale in a ring filled with our biggest, baddest superstars! I'm Steve, and this is my broadcast partner, Arthur.

ANNOUNCER 2: My name is certainly not Arthur. How many times do I have to tell you, it's…wait a minute, folks, I've just been informed that tonight will mark the debut of our newest competitor – from "parts unknown" – the devil!

A1: Hold on, ladies and gentlemen, it appears that The Crock has something to say.

THE CROCK (*loud macho voice*): Give me that microphone, jabronie. The Crock wants to say something to this "devil" clown. You think you're all big and scary. Well, The Crock isn't scared of you. That fire you've lived in for all these years doesn't compare to the heat you feel when you step into the ring with the great one! I've got Bulk Hogan, the Underfaker, and Oldberg watching my back. (*All of them do the "NWO" thing where they point at their friend sideways with one arm over their head, and one down by their side, like "he's the man."*) So come and get some, if you smell what I'm baking!

A2: Uh…Crock?

THE CROCK (*confused*): I mean, if you smell what I'm deep-frying…um…broiling…barbecuing?

BULK HOGAN (*normal voice*): Crock…it's cooking. If you smell what you're cooking.

THE CROCK (*normal voice*): Oh, right. Thanks, Bulk.

BULK HOGAN (*loud macho voice*): And whatcha gonna do, devil, when bulkamania runs all over you?!? Get out here!

THE DEVIL *runs out, looking scary. All the wrestlers look a bit shaken up by his appearance.*

A1: Bob, Lucifer definitely has the intimidation factor going here.

A2 (*annoyed at the name mix-up)*: Yes, that tends to happen when you're evil incarnate.

TD *wastes no time spearing* OLDBERG *down to the ground. As* OLDBERG *crawls offstage*, TD *throws* THE UNDERFAKER *out of the ring, and he too crawls offstage. He gives* HOGAN *a boot to the face, followed by a leg drop...and he too crawls offstage. As* THE CROCK *cowers in fear*, TD *gives him a "Rock Bottom," then drops the "People's Elbow." As* THE CROCK *crawls offstage*, THE DEVIL *celebrates in his mocking way, holding his hands to his ears as Hogan himself made famous*.

A1: Well, Charlie, it appears the prince of darkness has won the battle royale of our biggest superstars.

A2: And in his first ever WWF match! Not too shabby for someone with no known experience. This will definitely take the wind out of The Crock's sails.

A1: No doubt about that, Keith. I'm also pretty sure Hogan will never again claim to be the baddest wrestler in the world.

A2: Hold on, what's this? It appears we have ANOTHER newcomer in tonight's rumble!

A1: From…this must be somewhere overseas…the kingdom of Gad…

A2: Steve, you jabronie, it says "the Kingdom of God."

A1: That's what I said, Pete. Here comes the Christian!

THE CHRISTIAN *runs at* THE DEVIL *with a Bible in his hand.*

TC: I overcome you by the Blood of the Lamb, and the word of my testimony!

He whacks him over the head with the Bible.

A1: Ross, is that legal?

A2: It looks like they're allowing it!

TC: The One who is in me is greater than the one who is in the world!

He smacks him in the stomach.

TC: Resist the devil, and he must flee from you!

He knocks him to the ground, picks him up, and tosses him out the door.

TC: The Lord lives in me, and I have nothing to fear. Stay out of here, in Jesus' Name.

THE CHRISTIAN *then celebrates by doing a revised "NWO hand point" up to Heaven, representing giving the credit to God, his strength.*

A1: Andy, I've just been handed a piece of paper. "If God is for you, who can stand against you?"

A2: Apparently, not Satan. In fact, he won't be doing any standing at all for a long time.

A1 (*laughs uproariously*): HAHAHAHA. (*suddenly serious*) Good point, Tim.

A2: Steve, for the last time, my name is…

A1 (*interrupting*): And that's all the time we have for tonight, folks.

A1 and A2 together: Good night!

The End

MERCY IS FALLING

by Mike Massé

One of the main lessons I try to teach youth is that our actions have consequences. When we do make bad choices, however, God's mercy is there to forgive us and set us back on track.

CHARACTERS:
AUBREY – teen girl
TYLER – teen boy
JESS – teen girl
MALE PARAMEDIC
FEMALE PARAMEDIC
JESUS – should dress in a white robe if possible

PROPS: Various medical instruments: scalpel, forceps, incisors, etc. (These can all be mimed if nobody has access to them). The more medical stuff you have access to (doctor's breathing mask, etc.), the better.

AUBREY: Hey guys…come on in.

TYLER: This is so cool…your parents are gone for the weekend, and they left you the car!

JESS: Um…didn't they say you could only drive it to youth group?

AUBREY: Yeah, they said that. But won't this party we're going to have a group of youth there?

TYLER: So it's not even lying! You get to obey *and* tell the truth. Pastor Mike must be so proud he made us leaders in the youth group.

AUBREY: Yeah, we can just tell him we were visiting a different youth group to get some ideas for our next bring-a-friend event.

JESS: Wait a minute, guys. In every sketch we've ever done at church about a situation like this one there's a goody-goody friend that says, "Guys, I don't know about this."

TYLER: Are you that friend?

JESS: Of course not, I can't wait to party! Those sketches are so fake anyway…someone always dies and ends up sitting at the judgment seat of God.

AUBREY: And it's always some kid who had a friend that

was a Christian that never told them about Jesus. We're all Christian leaders at youth group, so we have nothing to worry about!

TYLER: Hey, Jess, remember that sketch when we were boyfriend and girlfriend?

JESS: Don't push it, buddy. Let's go!

They get in the car and head to the party. AUBREY *is driving crazy, and they are laughing about how, in the* sketch*, they'd be dead and in hell by now. Suddenly,* TYLER *sees headlights coming right at them.*

TYLER: Aubrey, look out!

AUBREY (*turned around toward the backseat*): Okay, Tyler, that was funny the first ten times...

JESS (*panicking*): He's serious, get out of the way!

JESS *tries to grab the wheel and swerve aside, but it is too late.* AUBREY *is immediately knocked unconscious and badly wounded.* TYLER *and* JESS *pull her out, lay her on the ground, and call an ambulance. All manner of joking has disappeared. They are devastated by the seriousness of possibly losing their friend. The ambulance pulls up and the paramedics put her on a gurney as the two teenagers huddle close for comfort. The male paramedic is a wanna-be doctor who will provide brief comic relief.*

JESS: I can't believe we were so stupid.

TYLER: It's my fault, it's my fault.

JESS: Please God, don't let her die.

TYLER: How can God even listen to us after the way we acted tonight?

MALE PARAMEDIC: Scalpel!

The FEMALE PARAMEDIC *hands him his scalpel.*

MP: Forceps!

She hands him his forceps.

MP: Incisors!

She hands him his incisors. He then stares at her blankly.

MP: Uh, all they ever say on the medical TV shows is scalpel… forceps…incisors. I don't know what comes next.

FP: Decide quickly, we're losing her!

MP: Okay. Give me the…um…things! (*mimes the AED paddles*)

FP: You mean the AED paddles?

MP: Yes, now!

She prepares the machine. He goes through the routine, rubbing the paddles together, yelling, "Clear!" and zapping AUBREY's *chest (for propriety's sake, he doesn't actually touch her). After several unsuccessful attempts, he shakes his head sadly, pulls the "covers" over her head, walks over to her friends, and pats* TYLER *on the shoulder.*

MP: I'm sorry, son. There's nothing more we can do.

TYLER: If it's okay with you, can we pray for her?

MP: Sure, son. Whatever makes you feel better.

TYLER *and* JESS *pray over* AUBREY's *body.*

JESS: Jesus, we know one of Your greatest gifts is mercy. We disobeyed, and I know that our actions have consequences. But we're sorry, and we're asking You for mercy.

TYLER: I know we don't deserve it at all, but please, Jesus, show us mercy and heal Aubrey completely.

They turn around, shaking their heads sadly. JESUS *walks out and puts his finger on* AUBREY's *forehead. She slowly sits up and gets out of bed. When* TYLER *and* JESS *turn back around, she is smiling with her arms spread wide. They embrace, and then begin to sing and dance (if it's possible, have a band or at least a drummer play the song).*

EVERYONE (*singing together*): Mercy is falling, is falling, is falling. Mercy is falling like a sweet spring rain. Mercy is falling is falling all over me! Hey-O I receive Your mercy, Hey-O, I receive Your grace. Hey-O I will dance forevermore!

The End

LOSER

by Mike Massé

Working with kids, you see words like "loser" thrown around all the time. It can be so easy to get discouraged when others put you down. The only way to avoid this is to see yourself as Jesus sees you. As the song says, only when we focus on Him do "the things of earth grow strangely dim in the light of His glory and grace."

CHARACTERS:
CHRISTIAN
DAN
MIKEY
JULIAN
SIGN CARRIER to walk by with signs

PROPS: Money, schoolbooks, signs with the names of all the weekdays on them, sign that says "Later that night, at Christian's house."

NOTE: This sketch is more enjoyable to the audience when the transitions are done really fast. We did the whole thing in about 3 minutes during one of our middle school "bring an unchurched friend" events. Christian would run out the "school" door and in through the "home" door (once out of sight, sprinting through the church halls), and they ate it up.

SIGN CARRIER *holds up the sign for* "MONDAY"

CHRISTIAN: Wow, youth group was great last night. We talked about how to witness to our friends. It sounded great. The only problem is…I wish I had some friends. Everyone in school thinks I'm a loser.

DAN, MIKEY, *and* JULIAN *walk by.*

DAN: Hey, look at that loser!

He points to Christian as his two friends laugh.

CHRISTIAN (*to audience*) See? They always talk at youth group about witnessing to your friends at school, but they never tell you how to make friends at school. I'm going to go home tonight and see what the Bible has to say about this. Then tomorrow, I'm going to have more friends than I can count!

SIGN CARRIER *holds up the "*Later that night, at Christian's house*" sign.*

CHRISTIAN (*reading*): Matthew 5:9 "Blessed are the peacemakers." Okay, I'll give it a try. By this time tomorrow, I'll be Mr. Social Skills!

SIGN CARRIER *holds up the sign for* "TUESDAY"

DAN, MIKEY, *and* JULIAN *walk by.*CHRISTIAN (*Holds up two fingers*) Peace, man.

DAN: Why don't you go back to the seventies where you belong? Actually, even back then, you'd still be a loser!

He points to Christian as his two friends laugh.

CHRISTIAN: Well, that didn't work. Maybe I need to look at a different place in the Bible. I'll check it out when I get home.

SIGN CARRIER *holds up the* "Later that night, at Christian's house" *sign.*

CHRISTIAN (*reading*): Luke 16:9 "I tell you, use worldly wealth to gain friends for yourself." Wow, why didn't I think of that before. Tomorrow, I'm bringing money to school. Soon, I'll be the President of Popular City!

SIGN CARRIER *holds up the sign for* "WEDNESDAY"

DAN, MIKEY, *and* JULIAN *walk by.*

CHRISTIAN: Hey guys, I'll give you $20 to be my friends.

DAN: Give me that! (*He snatches the money out of* CHRISTIAN'S *hand, then pushes him aside and walks away.*) Heh heh heh, thanks…loser!

CHRISTIAN: Well, the hippie thing didn't work, now bribes don't either. Something tells me I might be taking these Bible verses the wrong way.

SIGN CARRIER *holds up the* "Later that night, at Christian's house*" sign.*

CHRISTIAN (*reading*): Proverbs 25:22 "You will heap burning coals on his head."

He looks up at God, then at the audience, then shakes his head.

CHRISTIAN: Tempting, but no. Maybe I should read the verse before that. (*reading*) Proverbs 25:21 "If your enemy is hungry, give him food to eat." That's it! I'll kill him with kindness!

SIGN CARRIER *holds up the sign for* "THURSDAY."

CHRISTIAN is lying on the ground. DAN, MIKEY, *and* JULIAN *are walking away from him.*

DAN: I can't believe that loser tried to give me flowers and chocolates…what a freak show!

JULIAN: It *was* kind of thoughtful…(*he notices the other two staring at him incredulously*)…okay, okay, it was definitely weird, but he didn't mean anything by it. He just doesn't know how to act around people.

DAN: Because he's a loser!

CHRISTIAN: Wow, they're right. I don't know how to act around people. Tonight, I'm going to stop reading these random verses, and really ask God to help me.

SIGN CARRIER *holds up the* "Later that night, at Christian's house" *sign.*

CHRISTIAN: God, I really want to find a way to tell other kids about you. But how can I do it without them thinking I'm a loser? Please help me, God. Is there anything in here about being a loser? (*reading*) Matthew 10:39 "Whoever finds his life will lose it, and whoever loses his life for My sake will find it." (*Looks up like he just had an epiphany*) Wow, that's deep. All this time I've been worried about what they would think about me. What really matters is what Jesus thinks. All I can do is my best for God, and trust Him to take care of the rest. I can handle anything those kids say about me now!

SIGN CARRIER *holds up the sign for* "FRIDAY"

DAN, MIKEY *and* JULIAN *walk by.*

DAN: Hey, loser, what loser-ish thing are you going to do today?

CHRISTIAN: You wouldn't believe me if I told you.

DAN: Give it a try.

CHRISTIAN: I wanted to invite you guys to youth group Sunday night.

DAN *and* MIKEY *begin laughing at the top of their lungs.* JULIAN *looks curious.*

CHRISTIAN: Laugh all you want, I really don't care. But you guys are welcome to come check it out.

DAN: Yeah, right. Come on guys, let's let this loser go off to his loser group with all the other losers.

JULIAN: Actually, I want to find out more. I'll catch up with you guys later.

DAN *and* MIKEY *walk off.* JULIAN *turns to* CHRISTIAN.

CHRISTIAN: Are you serious? You really want to check out my youth group?

JULIAN: Yeah, you seem different today – like you really don't care what people think about you. I've always wanted that. I'll go with you…but on one condition.

CHRISTIAN: What's that?

JULIAN: Promise you'll never, ever show up again with flowers.

The End

HISTORY MAKER

by Mike Massé

By now, you've figured out that my sense of humor is a little different than that of the average churchgoer. This one was inspired at camp. The theme song that year was "History Maker" by Delirious, and I wanted to build around that. Jesus said, when talking about His works, that whoever had faith would accomplish even greater things...and we often forget this as we try to live in "the real world."

CHARACTERS:

MIKE

STEVE

PAUL – decked out in 'gangsta' garb…bandana, one pant leg pulled up, etc.

TIM – wearing athletic gear

NICK

T.J.

NARRATOR

PROPS: fake gun for Paul, gangsta outfit

TIM *stands frozen on one end of the stage*, PAUL *on the other.* STEVE *and* MIKE *stand in the middle of the stage. They are in a church. As the sketch opens*, STEVE *starts praising God, singing the song "History Maker" as* MIKE *looks on proudly.*

STEVE: I'm gonna be…a history maker in this land!

STEVE *abruptly stops singing and he freezes.* TIM *springs to life. He pantomimes dribbling and shooting a basketball.*

TIM: Man, I'm going to make history playing basketball. I'll be the best baller ever, way better than LeBron, AI, and even MJ! Look out world, I got more handle than a luggage rack full of suitcases! I'm so…OW MAN, AHH!

He falls to the ground, obviously in severe pain from a leg injury. He freezes on the ground, and PAUL *comes alive.*

PAUL: I'm gonna make history. I'm gonna be the illest gangsta ever…even better than Tupac! Oh man, I'm hardcore. I'm so hardcore, I'm going to kill the first person I see!

NICK *walks in with a resigned but content look on his face.* PAUL *doesn't hesitate to shoot him, and* NICK, *as expected, falls down dead.* T.J. *walks in behind* NICK, *and* PAUL *shoots* T.J. *in the leg. Even though it's clear he has been shot in the leg,* T.J. *grabs his own throat and takes a few last labored breaths before falling down dead.*

PAUL: Yeah yeah, I got the juice. Hmm…I think I'm going to pay a visit to that preacher that's always telling me about Jesus. I'll show him that I'm the only god around here. That will make history. Preacher will be praying to ME for mercy, that's hardcore.

PAUL *walks into the church where* MIKE *is engaging* STEVE *in some discipleship time. He points his gun at* MIKE.

PAUL: Hey yo, preach, who's the Lord now?

MIKE (*ignoring* PAUL, *talking to* STEVE): Time to practice God's Word in the real world. Do you remember that verse I taught you last week?

STEVE: Yes. "The son of Ham, the son of Cush, the son of Sabteca, the son of…

MIKE (*nervously interrupting*) No, no, not that one…the verse from Isaiah.

PAUL: Hurry it up, here.

STEVE: Oh yeah, Isaiah. "No weapon formed against me will prevail."

MIKE: No weapon formed against me will prevail. (*He puts his hand on the gun and slowly pushes it to the ground*).

PAUL (*humbled*): How can I be saved?

STEVE: Just ask, believe, and repent. Let's pray for Jesus to forgive you and be your Lord and Savior. Lord, save him.

All three make the sound that accompanies a revelation from above in commercials and sitcoms... "haaaaaaaaaaaaaaaaa aaaah" is the best way I can think of to spell it.

MIKE: Well, Paul, how does it feel to be saved?

PAUL: Phenomenal.

MIKE: Steve, we've been talking and singing about making history, now it's time to go do it! First, let's pray.

They lift their hands to Heaven and hear the same cherubic sound.

STEVE: Let's go make some history!

They exit the church and walk over to where TIM *is laying on the ground, still clutching his knee in pain.*

STEVE: What happened to you, man?

TIM: I don't know…I think I totally blew out my hamstring playing ball!

MIKE: Jesus said we'd do greater works than He did.

STEVE: And I know He healed a lot of people. (*Grabs* TIM's *hand*) Rise up and walk in the Name of Jesus. Now go jump around over there.

TIM *leaps to his feet and begins jumping around.*

TIM: Hallelujah, I'm healed!

The guys walk over to where the other two lie dead.

MIKE: Hey, look…some dead guys. What would Jesus do?

STEVE: Well, Jesus raised Lazarus from the dead. And… we're supposed to do greater things than Jesus.

MIKE: Let's make some history for God!

STEVE *looks at the two bodies.*

STEVE: The life of Jesus Christ…for you…rise up and come back to life!

The bodies leap back to life.

PAUL: Praise the Lord! You raised Nick from the dead! (*audience cheers like crazy*)

NARRATOR: Zechariah 4:6 – "Not by might, nor by power, but by My Spirit," says the Lord Almighty.

The End

NO OTHER GODS

3 - Part Movie Parody Series

Part 1

CHAPEL OF THE APES

by Mike Massé and TJ Steele

CHARACTERS:

APES – 4 or 5 of them

APE PASTOR

CHRISTIAN

NARRATOR

PROPS: Inflatable monkey (can be found online for a few bucks), banana, hymnal.

NARRATOR (*reading*): Exodus 20:3 – You shall have no other gods before me…even on the "Planet of the Apes."

4 or 5 APES *sit in their seats at church...making ape-like noises, scratching themselves, etc. The* APE PASTOR *stands in front of them, and prepares to start the church service.*

AP: Welcome, everyone to the Planet of the Apes Community Church. As you know, we have developed into super-intelligent, super-strong…super-apes. We worship our own race (*he points to the inflatable monkey that hangs on the wall of the church*), and the mighty banana that sustains us. If everyone can turn in your hymnals to number 30…

ALL APES SING: "Hmmm…Come on Mr. Tally-man, tally me banana…6 foot 7 foot 8 foot bunch!"

AP: Ah, that's one of my favorites. Does anybody have a testimony they'd like to share?

APE 1 *stands up and makes some shrieking noises.* APE 2 *jumps up next to him and begins to shriek as well.*

AP: Yes, we all rejoice that the ape upstairs has driven out all the fruit flies. We will now pass the communion banana.

As the APE PASTOR *reaches behind him and picks up the banana,* CHRISTIAN *runs in and grabs the inflatable monkey. He wrestles it to the ground and drops a couple of elbows, making sure the last one pops it. He holds up the pathetic remains, as the apes stare in amazement.*

CHRISTIAN: What do you think of your god now, ape?

All the APES *gasp.*

AP: How can you, a human, talk, as we advanced beings do? And how did you escape from your cage?

CHRISTIAN: Question one: I've always been able to talk, I've just been waiting until the right time. Question two (*pauses dramatically*): It was unlocked.

AP: Of course! But once you escaped, why did you come to our church instead of running away?

CHRISTIAN: Because God…the one true God…sent me with a message!

AP: And what is this message?

CHRISTIAN: God loves you.

AP: Me?

CHRISTIAN: You.

AP: Me?

CHRISTIAN: You.

AP: Me?

CHRISTIAN: You.

AP: Me?

CHRISTIAN (*trying to contain his impatience*): Listen, monkey, God loves everyone…even a dirty, ugly, foul, smelly ape like you!

AP: And you're telling me this is…good news?

CHRISTIAN: Yes, it's great news. The best news anyone could ever receive!

AP: And I suppose we have to give up bananas?

CHRISTIAN: No, you can still eat as many as you want! But you do have to stop worshipping false gods.

AP: How can we be saved?

CHRISTIAN: Well, this is where it gets weird. The Bible was written years before the concept of super-intelligent apes came into existence. But all humans have to do is admit their sin, ask Jesus to change their hearts, and start following Him!

AP: Yet there are still millions of humans who don't know this!

CHRISTIAN: How do you know this?

AP: Well, it's not as dramatic as finding the remains of the Statue of Liberty…but, um, this isn't some faraway planet. It's Earth.

CHRISTIAN: (*shouting*) NOOOOOOOOOOOOOO! (*immediately calms down*) Wait, yes. I knew that. You actually captured me in the parking lot of that mall right over there (*points to the mall*). If you don't mind, I have to go finish my Christmas shopping.

AP: Yes, Christian, off you go. Spread the word about this God of yours.

CHRISTIAN: I'll do that. This has been more fun than a barrel of…well, you know.

As CHRISTIAN *sprints off, the apes clap him on the back, wishing him well.*

The End

NO OTHER GODS

3 - Part Movie Parody Series

Part 2
THE FAST AND THE IDOLATROUS

by Mike Massé and TJ Steele

CHARACTERS:

MIKE

KYLE

NICK – (*a recurring character who always died a la "Kenny"*)

PAUL – (*a recurring character who always commented on Nick's passing*)

APE PASTOR

NARRATOR

PROPS: It works best if all vehicles are mimed.

NARRATOR (*reading*): Exodus 20:3 – You shall have no other gods before me…even during "The Fast and the Furious."

MIKE *stands in the middle of the stage, waiting for his friends.*

MIKE: I can't wait for my friends to get here so we can start street racing.

PAUL *pulls up in his old car.*

MIKE: Hey, Paul. You really think you have a chance to beat me with this old bucket?

PAUL: Eh, probably not. At least I'm in better shape than Nick. His mom grounded him from the car for a month.

MIKE: The Avenger? When was that?

PAUL: Twenty-nine days ago.

MIKE: Wow, I really need to start paying closer attention when he talks. So he gets his sweet car back tomorrow…what's he going to race with tonight?

PAUL: Um…I think he said his bike.

MIKE: The Ducati?

PAUL: No, his dad grounded him from that too. I think he meant his "bike" bike.

MIKE (*incredulous*): The ten-speed?!?!

PAUL: Dude, Kyle is bringing his brand new Corvette. We all might as well be racing with ten-speeds.

Both point and stare as KYLE *pulls up in his hot car. At that exact moment, ringing the little handlebar bell,* NICK *rides by on his bike. He is promptly run over.*

PAUL: Oh my goodness, you killed Nick! Hey, sweet ride.

KYLE: You bet it is.

MIKE: Yeah, that car is hot. But does it have NOS?

KYLE: Oh, it has NOS, all right. All the NOS you can handle.

PAUL: You can never have too much NOS.

KYLE: Well, this car is all about the NOS.

PAUL: NOS.

KYLE (*nodding*): NOS.

NICK (*leans up on one arm to say the line, looks impressed, then collapses again*): Dude, sweet NOS!

They look at him for a second, shake their heads, then turn their attention back to the Corvette.

KYLE: I can't even tell you how much I love this thing. This car is like a god to me.

PAUL: I can't think of anything else more deserving of worship.

MIKE: Well, boys, ready for some street racing action?

KYLE: Of course…but where's your car?

MIKE: Dang, I knew I forgot something! Do you think Nick will mind if I borrow his bike?

KYLE: Well, you'll have about as much chance as Paul does of beating me. What with all my…

MIKE: If you say "NOS" one more time…

KYLE: Okay, okay – let's do this!

All three head up to the starting line. KYLE *is revving his engine,* PAUL *tries to reciprocate, but hears only sputtering.* MIKE *is humorously ringing the bell in a pointless attempt to intimidate the competition. The race begins.* MIKE *is going at top speed, and* PAUL *is alongside him at the same rate.*

PAUL: I wonder why the speedometer even goes to 85. Once I pass 30, the whole front end starts shaking.

KYLE *mockingly keeps his car next to theirs.*

KYLE: Well boys, time to flip a little switch I lovingly call "the NOS activator." Eat my proverbial dust!

MIKE: Wait a minute…is that a banana in his tailpipe?

KYLE *flips the switch, and the car immediately explodes as the three of them dive to safety. When the dust clears, the* APE PASTOR *is standing over them.*

PAUL: Oh, man, it's one of those super-intelligent apes.

MIKE: I hate them! Always putting people in cages…

AP: Silence! (*beat*) What do you think of your idol now, human?

KYLE: I guess my car wasn't so god-like after all.

AP: No, there is only one true God. One of your own told me the good news yesterday.

ALL THREE: How can we be saved?

AP: I'm going to tell you the story about God and His only Son.

KYLE: Son? That's "NOS" backwards!

ALL THREE: Tell us more!

The End

NO OTHER GODS

3 - Part Movie Parody Series

Part 3
FORREST AWAY

by Mike Massé

CHARACTERS:

FORREST GUMP – says all of his lines in his slow Southern drawl

NICK – (*a recurring character who always died a la "Kenny"*)

PAUL – (*a recurring character who always commented on Nick's passing*)

KYLE

APE PASTOR

NARRATOR

PROPS: volleyball (*make sure it says "Spalding" or anything but "Wilson" on it*).

NARRATOR (*reading*): Exodus 20:3 – You shall have no other gods before me…even if "Forrest Gump" gets "Cast Away."

FORREST GUMP *is lying on the ground. He gets up and looks around slowly, taking in his surroundings.*

FG (*rubbing his head*): Ouch. That was painful. Jen-nay always said "run, Forrest, run." But I think it was a bad idea to run out of a hot air balloon making a trip across the ocean. Now I appear to be on a deserted island somewhere. I'm like a castaway. I don't see Bubba, or momma, or any Dr. Pepper, or choc-o-lates. At least I'll have all the shrimp I can eat. Did someone say shrimp? I love shrimp. Shrimp cocktail, shrimp kabobs, shrimp scampi…and a big bowl of oatmeal with milk, and on the side…some shrimp. What do we have here?

He sees a volleyball on the ground and picks it up.

FG: I wonder how this got here. You need a name. I think I'll call you…(*Looks at the "Spalding" on the side of the ball*). "Wilson." Wilson, you're the best friend I've ever had since I've been cast away on this deserted island. Wilson…I think I'm going to worship you.

NICK *comes walking through the waters of low tide.*

NICK: I'm here to save you!

FG: Look out for that tidal wave.

NICK *looks up at the tidal wave bearing down on him and disappears underneath it.* PAUL *surfs by on a board.*

PAUL: Oh my goodness, you killed Nick!

FG: That was interesting. Wilson, now that you're a god, couldn't you have saved that man? Why don't you answer me? Why is there a helicopter landing over there?

There is indeed a helicopter landing on the island. The APE PASTOR flies it and KYLE *is a passenger. They both hop out and walk over to* FORREST.

FG: A gorilla flying a helicopter. Now I've seen everything.

APE PASTOR: I was going to say the same thing about a man talking to a volleyball.

KYLE: Listen, we're on a mission to tell everyone about the one true God. We saw you worshipping your volleyball. Let me tell you, up until yesterday, I used to worship my car…and although it made more sense than a volleyball…it was still an idol that left me empty and disappointed. Then my friend here, the chimp…

FG (*interrupting*): Did you say shrimp?

KYLE: No, <u>chimp</u>. This super-intelligent ape here.

FG: Makes sense.

KYLE: Anyway, he told me about Jesus, and He's my God now, and it's amazing.

FG: How can I be saved?

KYLE: You can start by sending that idol where it belongs!

FORREST *hits Wilson as hard as he can out into the ocean, never to be seen again.*

AP (*to Wilson*): You just got served!

KYLE: Good one, monkey! Now lets close with one of those song and dance numbers everyone loves!

EVERYONE (*singing and dancing like crazy*): There is no god like Jehovah…there is no god like Jehovah…there is no god like Jehovah…there is no god like Je-ho-o-vah!

The End

SIN IS STUPID

by Steve Kaplan and Dave Waite

A simple object lesson about how teenagers view worldliness. Both characters speak with very exaggerated inflections, over-the-top nodding (for yes and no) and animated hand motions to punctuate their dialogue. This sketch is best when spread out over the course of a service, or a we originally did it, each afternoon at camp.

CHARACTERS:

NUMBER 1

NUMBER 2

EXTRAS – 4 audience members (minimal preparation needed) for Act II.

PROPS: Tickle-Me-Elmo doll

ACT I - SCUBA DIVING

1: I wonder who I can get today. Hey look…there's an idiot!

2: Me?

1: Yes…you!

2: All right!

1: Do you…want to go…scuba diving?

2: No…(*turn away, then back*)

1 and 2: YES!

1: In the Atlantic…Ocean

2: I love the Atlantic! Aren't you going to give me some air?

1: Yes! 2 TANKS!

2: I love 2 tanks of oxygen.

1: …Nitrogen!

2: But isn't that kind of dangerous?

1: Yes! But don't worry…we're going to strap you with C4!

2: Yes! I love C! And I love 4!

1: And when you can't breathe anymore, just press the button.

2: …so tell me, have you ever done this before?

1: No!

2: Has anyone ever done this before?

1: No!

2: So you're telling me there's a chance I might die?

1: No…(*turn away, then back*)

1 and 2: Yes!

2: What are the chances I might live?

1: ZERO PERCENT!

2: Yes! I love those kinds of odds. (*pause*) So tell me, do I get paid?

1: No!

2: So what I do get out of it?

1: You get to be cool!

2: You mean you'll think I'm cool?

1: Yes!

2: Yes! I've always wanted to be cool!

1 and 2 (*out of character, to audience*): Sin…is stupid.

ACT II - 3 LEGGED RACE

1: I wonder who I can get today. Hey look…there's an idiot!

2: Me?

1: Yes…you!

2: All right!

1: Do you…want to do a 3-legged race…across a…10-lane highway?

2: No…(*turn away, then back*)

1 and 2: YES!

2: But…it's a 3-legged race…and I only have 2 legs!

1: That's okay…I've got a partner for you! (*Pulls out a Tickle-Me-Elmo doll*)

2: All right! But isn't that still kind of dangerous?

1: Yes! But doesn't he look happy?

2: Yes! Then I shall be happy!

AUDIENCE MEMBERS 1-4 *stand up and say their line, one after another.*

AM1: Then I shall be happy!

AM2: Then I shall be happy!

AM3: Then I shall be happy!

AM4: Then I shall be happy!

2: …so tell me, have you ever done this before?

1: No!

2: Has anyone ever done this before?

1: No!

2: So you're telling me there's a chance I might die?

1: No…(*turn away, then back*)

1 and 2: Yes!

2: What are the chances I might live?

1: ZERO PERCENT!

2: Yes! I love those kinds of odds. So tell me, do I get paid?

1: No! But…he does! (*Points to Elmo doll*)

2: So what I do get out of it?

1: You get to be cool!

2: You mean you'll think I'm cool?

1: Yes!

2: Yes! I've always wanted to be cool!

1 and 2 (*out of character, to audience*): Sin…is stupid.

ACT III - RUSSIAN ROULETTE

1: I wonder who I can get today. Hey look…there's an idiot!

2: Me?

1: Yes…you!

2: All right!

1: Have you ever played with…guns?

2: No…(*turn away and set up for YES!)*

2 (*turn back, switch to normal voice and mannerisms for both*): Actually, no, I haven't.

1: Really? You never went to Boy Scout camp? Toy BB gun? Paintball? Nothing? You ever saw them on TV? Yeah? But you never played with them?

1 (*Crazy voices again for both*): Well…do you want to?

2: Yes!

1: All right! I have a game for you called Russian…Roulette!

2: Russian? Well…G'day mate! Toss another shrimp on the Barbie!

1: And to make it really great, I'm going to put 6 bullets…in 6 chambers!

2: All right! So what are the chances I might live?

1: ZERO PERCENT!

2: Yes! I love those kinds of odds. So tell me, do I get paid?

1: No!

2: So what I do get out of it?

1: You get to be cool!

2: You mean you'll think I'm cool?

1: Yes!

2: Yes! I've always wanted to be cool!

1 and 2 (*out of character, to audience*): Sin…is stupid.

The End

SUSIE Q

by Mike Massé

This was my first Christian "full-length" drama. I have seen it work effectively with various audiences...church youth groups, community kids at a concert, and even prospective youth pastors at a ministry college. Definitely for high school kids, some themes are too mature for middle school or younger. I usually fade the lights completely out and in again to transition between scenes, with "outdoor" (beach) and "indoor" (church and school) sides of the stage.

CHARACTERS:

SUSIE Q – teen girl
JOHNNY GQ – "cool" teen boy
MIKE – youth pastor
BODHI – teen boy
MINDY – adult leader of a youth 'small group'
LEESAH – teen girl
CRAIG – teen boy
JERVACIO – teen boy
TINY TOM – should be a good-sized person with sneakers on their knees, making them appear 3 feet tall.
ANNETTE – older teen girl

DAVID – teen boy
LLOYD – teen boy
HEATHER – teen girl
EXTRAS – YOUTH GROUP MEMBERS

PROPS: chairs for the church and classroom
OPTIONAL (Can be pantomimed): surfboards, a "fire," musical soundtrack

---

NARRATOR: Susie Q. was a normal high school freshman. She got decent grades at school, went to the occasional party, but basically stayed out of trouble. She was pretty content with her life, but recently she had been feeling a little depressed. As she entered high school, her guidance counselor had asked what she wanted to do with her life. Susie had no answer. It wasn't that she was so concerned with finding an occupation, but the fact that she suddenly felt useless…like her life had no purpose whatsoever. She started to question whether there was more to life than just going to school and hanging out with her friends. As August came to an end, though, she just wanted to enjoy the beach and the guys that were surfing right in front of her.

SCENE 1: On the beach, full light

SUSIE Q. *watches* MIKE *and a member of his recreation team,* BODHI, *surfing. As they ride the last wave back to shore, she approaches them.*

SUSIE: Hey man, you've got some pretty cool moves…

MIKE: Well, thanks.

SUSIE: …for an old guy.

MIKE: Hey, I'm 24 years old!

SUSIE: Like I said.

BODHI: Ooh…that's rough.

MIKE: So what are you up to tonight?

SUSIE: Nothing special. What are you two doing?

MIKE: Well, I'm glad you asked. We're headed to a concert at the church down the street. We do it every Sunday night. It's where a bunch of middle and high schoolers meet to talk, sing a few songs, basically just hang out. It's nothing like church as you probably think of it.

SUSIE: Yeah, I heard a few kids at school talking about those meetings.

MIKE: We're actually heading over right now.

BODHI: You're more than welcome to come check it out.

SUSIE: Well, I've got nothing better to do.

MIKE: Come on. (*They begin walking to the fire.*) My name's Mike, by the way. This is Bodhi.

Susie: I'm Susie. Susie Q.

Scene 2 – indoor, full light to dim when the music starts,* EXTRAS *in conversation

They arrive at the meeting, and MIKE *greets a few* YOUTH GROUP MEMBERS, *and subtly introduces* SUSIE *to small group leader* MINDY, *who introduces* SUSIE *to some other freshmen. An upbeat song begins to play, and everyone sings and claps.*

NARRATOR: Susie was touched by the obvious passion for God and life that the band put into their songs. She noticed the way the youth group interacted with each other, and how the older students all seemed at peace…like they had purpose in their lives. At the end of the night, the worship leader asked if there was anybody there who wanted to accept and start following Jesus. Susie made that decision and asked Mindy to pray with her. Four weeks go by, and all of Susie's friends notice a change in her attitude. She has attended every Sunday night meeting, and even has begun inviting other people to come. She is anxious to share her newfound morals with her classmates, and she got that chance Wednesday morning in current events class. Unfortunately, her class was less than thrilled…Susie was the only one in her class to feel that abortion was wrong. Discouraged, she decided to see if Mindy had any advice for her.

Scene 3 – indoor, small group sitting in a circle with Mindy leading, full light

MINDY: Welcome to our discussion group, the topic tonight is, "Today's tough issues." Remember that it's an open forum, and everything we say here is confidential. Who wants to start?

SUSIE: Can we talk about abortion? We've been discussing it in current events class, and I've really been made to look foolish. They call me every name from 'moron' to 'close-minded right-wing bigoted freak.' Is there anything in the Bible to defend my position?

MINDY: The best verse on that subject is Psalm 139:13, which states that God knew us while we were being formed in our mothers' wombs. Try telling your class that. Before you leave tonight, we will all pray for you to have boldness. Plus I've got a secret weapon for you…I went to college with a certain celebrity before he became famous. He owes me a favor…let's see if he doesn't mind paying a visit to your school tomorrow.

NARRATOR: With her newfound wisdom, the prayers of her discipleship group, and Mindy's secret weapon, Susie heads to current events class the next day. The heated debate soon resumes.

Scene 4 – Indoor, classroom, students at desks, full light

LEESAH: So, is Susie the Flying Nun still anti-choice?

SUSIE (*confidently*): Yes, actually, God says in the Bible that He knew us while we were still in our mother's womb. It's also been medically proven that a fetus starts to have human characteristics as young as 9 weeks (****of course, use the latest medical statistic)*.

CRAIG: Who believes that crap, anyway?

SUSIE: Well…how about Tiny Tom, famous Hollywood midget! (TINY TOM *waddles into the room*).

CRAIG and JERVACIO: NO WAY!!!!!

TINY TOM: If my mom had had an abortion when she was pregnant with me, where would you all be?

JERVACIO: I don't even want to think about it.

LEESAH: A world without "Tiny Tom Saves the Farm Part III" would be a scary world indeed.

CRAIG: Maybe you have a point after all

SUSIE (*to God*): Thank you, Lord.

NARRATOR: Susie finished her freshman year strong. She began to be known around school as being truly sincere and reaching out to people. But summer brought a new boyfriend into her life...and as her sophomore year progresses, she has something to confess to her discussion group.

Scene 5: Indoor, discussion group sitting in chairs. Full light.

MINDY: What was it that you wanted to share, Susie?

SUSIE: I, well, you know, went too far physically with Johnny GQ the other night.

MINDY: I went through the same thing with Jason back in high school. He loved God as much as I did, and together we kept ourselves accountable...and now we've been married for five incredible years. But I know Johnny doesn't know God, so it's a whole different story. Annette, do you want to share anything to share with Susie?

ANNETTE: Susie, I went through the same exact thing with Eddie Details last summer. And it was through this group that God helped me overcome my temptation. The verse that really brought me through was, "God won't let you be tempted beyond what you can bear." And the prayers of my friends really made me feel strong enough to stop seeing Eddie.

MINDY: Why don't we pray for Susie right now?

ANNETTE: And I'll call you Saturday morning to see how things went.

NARRATOR: Susie had made her decision. With her group's help, she had made a commitment to stop this behavior. That Friday night, she got a great chance to test that commitment when she and Johnny GQ were on the beach alone.

Scene 6: Outdoor, beach, one dim light, possible Aerosmith love song in background

JOHNNY: You know what I want to do right now?

SUSIE: Roast marshmallows?

JOHNNY: Susie, you're so crazy. C'mere (*leans in to kiss her*).

SUSIE (*pulls away*): Johnny, I can't do this any more.

JOHNNY: Why, what's the problem? Does this have anything to do with that religious stuff you're always talking about?

SUSIE: It's not religion; it's my relationship with my Savior.

JOHNNY: Remember when I asked you why you love everybody so much?

SUSIE: Yeah, I told you it is because God is love.

JOHNNY: Well, why don't we express our love for each other? (*leans in again*)

SUSIE (*standing up*): Johnny, you don't love me.

JOHNNY: Maybe not, but I have honestly never felt this way about a girl before.

SUSIE: I really do care about you, and still want to see you. Just not alone.

JOHNNY: Oh, so now you don't trust me.

SUSIE: No, I don't trust myself, not yet. And I'll be praying for you (*She walks away*).

JOHNNY (*to himself*): I hate to see her leave, but I love to watch her go.

NARRATOR: God used that discussion group to bring Susie to the next level of Christian maturity. Let's now jump ahead to her senior year. Susie was already involved in some ministry, mostly stuff that involved people…such as becoming a member of the surfing team that had helped draw her to the group in the first place. She also was so influenced by her mentor, Annette, that she became one herself during senior year. She was now following Jesus with everything she had. But because she was going to graduate in a couple of months, she began to desperately wish to see members of her class learn the truth about Jesus. She had seen commitments begin and fade, and she wanted to learn how to effectively convince them of God's purpose for their lives.

Scene 7: Outdoor, Beach at night, one dim light, possible soft rock music in background until Johnny approaches, when the music will fade out

SUSIE: Don't you ever wonder if there's more to this life than partying every weekend, wasting all your money just to make a fool out of yourself?

DAVID: Dude, if there's something better than drinking until I pass out with some chick I've never met before, I don't want to hear about it.

SUSIE: Well, what about eternal life? Where do you think you go when you die?

LLOYD: Man, the way I see it, when you die, you are dead. Done, gone, dust, nothing else.

SUSIE: But think about it! If Heaven and hell don't exist, you have nothing to lose. If they do, you have everything to gain!

LLOYD: Nothing to lose? How about alcohol, sex, my so-called "satanic" music – the only things that make this pointless life worth living. No thanks.

DAVID: Yeah, Susie, if I went to hell, I would kick the devil in the head, and take over his kingdom. Soon, I would conquer Heaven, too. Yeah, that would rule.

HEATHER (*quietly*): What must I do to be saved?

SUSIE: (*overjoyed*) Are you really ready to make this life-changing decision?

HEATHER: No, I was kidding. I'm an atheist, you moron. Let's go back to the party, guys.

DAVID (*rapping, fades as they walk away*): It's getting hot in here! So take off all…

SUSIE (*praying, noticeably sad*): God, I know you never force anybody to change their lives. But when you gave humans freedom of choice, did you know they were going to be so stubborn, so…stupid about changes that would give them a reason to live?

She stops and turns around, noticing her old friend JOHNNY *slowly walking towards her.*

JOHNNY: Hey, stranger.

SUSIE: Did you hear anything I just said?

JOHNNY: Yeah, the whole "salvation" message. (*sadly sarcastic*) "Jesus loves you and He died for your sins."

SUSIE: What do you think?

JOHNNY: You know I've never believed God could love me because of all the crappy things that have happened to me. (*Visibly in pain*) If God loved me, why did my mom abandon me? Why did my drunken dad allow my little brother to go swimming in the storm the day he drowned? I always thought love was a myth, Susie.

SUSIE (*almost in tears*): Johnny, I know you've been through so much. Remember how I always told you that stuff isn't God…that the devil, for now, rules this world. God can intervene, but He chose to give humans free choice.

JOHNNY: Right, God does not rule this world. But He rules you, Susie. And you're the most loving person I've ever met in my life. You've made it a point to love me. Of all the girls I've ever been with, you were the only one who came to see me after my car accident. Yeah, they all call constantly on party nights, but you called after my brother died, when I was going through emotional hell. Ever since freshman year, you've said that God was your life. I've seen it, Susie. I want to know what incredible love could drive you to care about a jerk like me. I want to know God.

SUSIE (*crying, if you can pull it off, otherwise just very emotional):* Pray with me, Johnny.

Lights out, tears, thunderous applause . . .

The End

LET ME GO

Based on the concept from the church skit "Entertaining Jesus/Stay Here," author unknown. Revised characters and dialogue by Mike Massé

I learned the original skit while training a youth missions team, and loved the ending. I can't take credit for the powerful revelation here...and I've searched far and wide to locate the sketch's original creator, only to come up short every time.

This one definitely needs a strong lead actor. The point being made is what is missing in many youth groups – a daily walk with Christ in the real world. I changed the characters, modified the situation to make it relevant to today's youth, added some funny lines...and kept what I believe is the best "knockout punch" ending ever.

THE MOST IMPORTANT THING: People are going to laugh at the end when Christian tries to leave and Jesus keeps following him. Christian needs to be light and funny the first time he leads Him back into the room, and get angrier each time...ratchet up the intensity without any comic relief. If done right, it's jaw-dropping.

CHARACTERS:

CHRISTIAN

JESUS – In this version, He never utters a word

MEGAN

MATT

RYAN

SOMEONE – to be offstage, make a phone ring, and tap a microphone twice

PROPS: A telephone, a couch (2 chairs can be substituted), a television with remote control, a Bible covered with dirt to be blown off, representing having never been read

---

CHRISTIAN (*kneeling in prayer*): Dear Jesus, I really felt bad when I heard my youth leader talk about living as a witness in the real world. I haven't really done that, and he said it was because I only walked with you during youth group on Sundays, and not the rest of the week. I'm sorry for doing that, Jesus. Today is Saturday, and I want to ask You to walk with me today, Jesus. I ask you to be with me in everything I do today, and help me live a life of character, and be a good witness for You. Amen.

CHRISTIAN *gets up and looks around. Suddenly, he smiles as he sees* JESUS *walk up and stand next to him.*

CHRISTIAN: Hey, Jesus, good to see you! I knew You'd come.

JESUS *just smiles at him.*

CHRISTIAN: So, this is really cool, huh? Walking with Jesus. Crazy stuff, having the Creator and Savior of the world right here in my living room. Pretty awesome, though. This is the first time we've ever hung out outside of church. So, um…what do you want to do?

JESUS *just smiles at him.*

CHRISTIAN: Hmm, I suppose you leave the decisions up to me. How about some guidance? Well, You probably want me to read the Bible.

CHRISTIAN *picks up his Bible and blows the 'dust' off of it.*

CHRISTIAN (*embarrassed*): Oh, that's not dust! It's just falling apart from me reading it so much.

JESUS *looks at him intently.*

CHRISTIAN: Man, Jesus, You've been here 2 minutes, and already I'm lying to You. It's not easy having You right here with me. I'll try to be straight with You from now on.

JESUS *smiles and motions to the Bible.*

CHRISTIAN: Okay…let's see…what do we have here. John 15:16, "You have not chosen me, but I have chosen you to bear fruit…fruit that will last." Hmm…I wonder what that means. Oh, are You trying to tell me You're hungry? I'll go grab You an apple from the kitchen.

As CHRISTIAN *gets up, the phone rings.* JESUS *follows him wherever he goes, staying about 2 feet away at all times, never taking His eyes off* CHRISTIAN.

CHRISTIAN: Hello?

MATT: Hey man, it's Matt. You coming to the party later?

CHRISTIAN: Well, I kind of have a guest here.

MATT: Someone from school?

CHRISTIAN: No, He's from, um…out of town. Bethlehem… Pennsylvania!

MATT: So, ask if He wants to come!

CHRISTIAN: I don't think He's into that sort of party. I'll see you Monday.

CHRISTIAN *hangs up the phone and they walk back into the living room.*

CHRISTIAN: That was pretty holy of me, huh Jesus? Refusing that sinful party like that. High five!

JESUS *puts His hand on* CHRISTIAN'S *shoulder, and they sit down on the couch.*

CHRISTIAN: Hmm, what can we do? What do You say we watch a little TV?

He turns the TV on, and begins switching channels.

CHRISTIAN: Sweet, MTV! Music has come a long way since Your day, huh Jesus?

JESUS *looks at him sadly.*

CHRISTIAN: Oh, right, you don't want to watch this. Let's see what else is on. Wow, the Baywatch reunion special! Look at that lifeguard run...(*he sees* JESUS *looking away*)...run right off that screen! I am shocked and appalled at what passes for entertainment these days!

He flicks the TV off.

CHRISTIAN: I know! We can play Bible trivia!

The doorbell rings.

CHRISTIAN: Oh, I'd better get that. I guess we'll have to wait to play Bible trivia...well, You'd probably whup me anyway.

JESUS *follows* CHRISTIAN *to the door. He opens it.*

MATT: Hey, C-diddy, we thought you might have changed your mind and wanted to come to the party with us.

RYAN: Yeah, dawg, let's get going!

CHRISTIAN: I don't know, guys.

MATT: Don't tell me that youth group is making you into some kind of holy freak.

CHRISTIAN: It's not that, it's just...

RYAN: Did we forget to tell you, Megan is going to be there!

CHRISTIAN: Megan!

RYAN: Yeah, she's right here waiting in the car.

MEGAN: Hi, Christian!

CHRISTIAN: Excuse me for a second. (*Takes* JESUS *by the hand and leads Him back into the room*). Hey, Jesus, I changed my mind about that party. I think I'm going to go and tell all the kids there about You. Yeah, that's it. I can't really be a witness hanging around here all day. I really need to go witness to that girl in the car. I know I said I wanted to hang out, but it will be better if You just <u>let me go</u>. Why don't you play that Bible trivia game with my sister…she thinks she's so smart, I bet she doesn't even score against You! As much fun as we've had, I'm going to have to ask you to <u>let me go</u>. Bye, Jesus.

He walks to the door. JESUS *follows right behind him.*

CHRISTIAN: Uh, I have to take care of one more thing, guys. (*He takes* JESUS *back to the couch and sits Him down*). Okay, Jesus, I know I asked You to walk with me today, and it's been great, but I'm trying to tell You that You really won't like this party. Just <u>LET ME GO.</u>

He walks back to the door. JESUS *follows right behind him.*

CHRISTIAN: Hold on, guys.

RYAN: What is taking you so long, man? Megan is waiting!

MEGAN: Come sit next to me, Christian.

CHRISTIAN: I PROMISE I will be right out! (*Grabs* JESUS' *wrist and leads him back to the couch impatiently*). Jesus, I told You to let me go. I'm starting to get a little impatient. Just LET ME GO!

He walks to the door angrily. JESUS follows right behind him.

CHRISTIAN (*furiously grabs* JESUS' *arms, and "nails" them one at a time to the "Cross"*) (***NOTE:*** *if someone who is not in the sketch can tap a microphone as each nail hits each wrist, the effect is amazing)*: JESUS! How many times do I have to tell you: LET ME (*nail*), GO (*nail*)!

As JESUS stands there "crucified" and in pain, CHRISTIAN takes one last look at Him, then hurries out the door.

The End

Printed in the United States
34301LVS00002B/175-240